CANDY WORLD

24 PAGE COLORING BOOK

Illustrations by Dani Kates

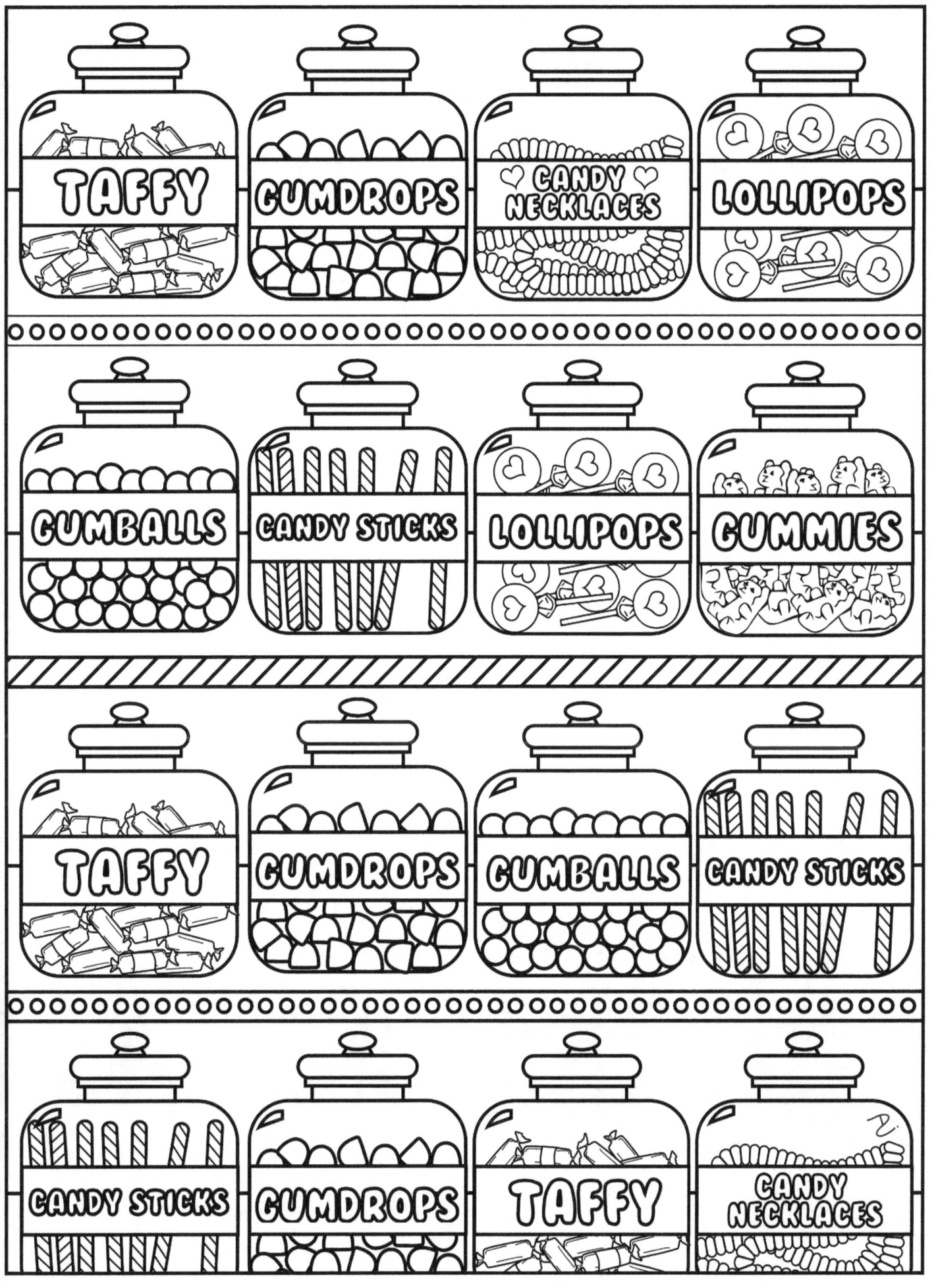

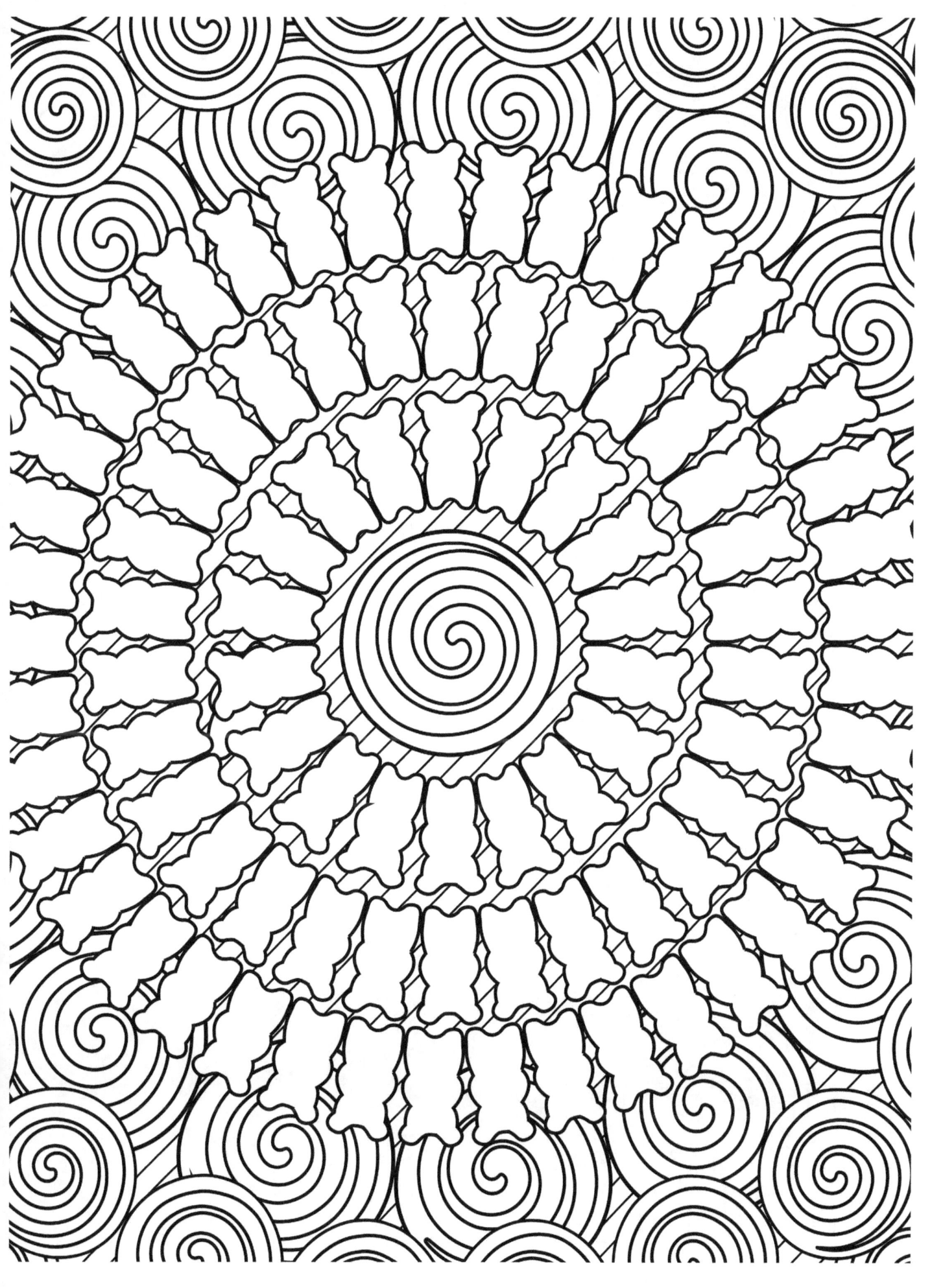

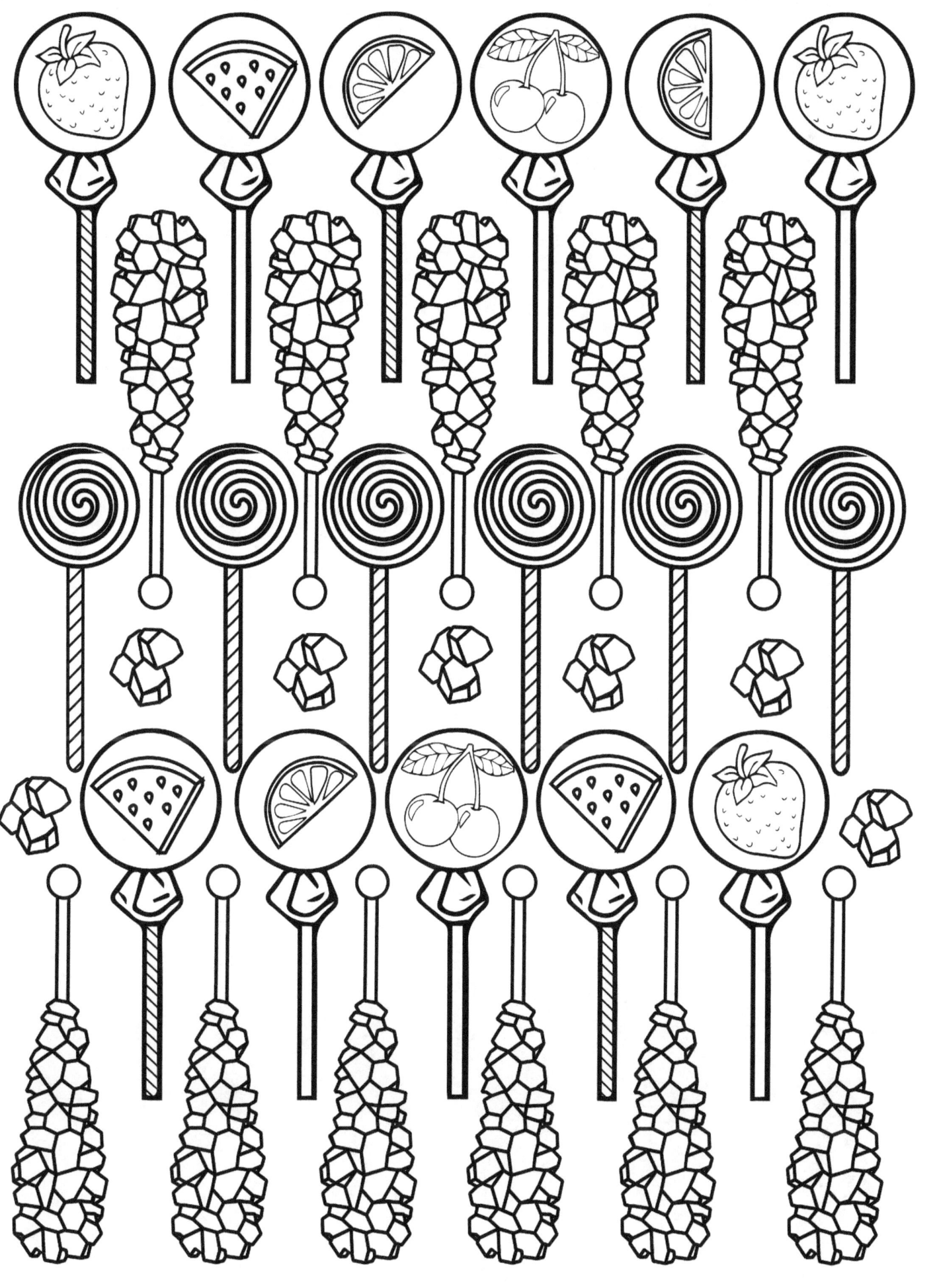

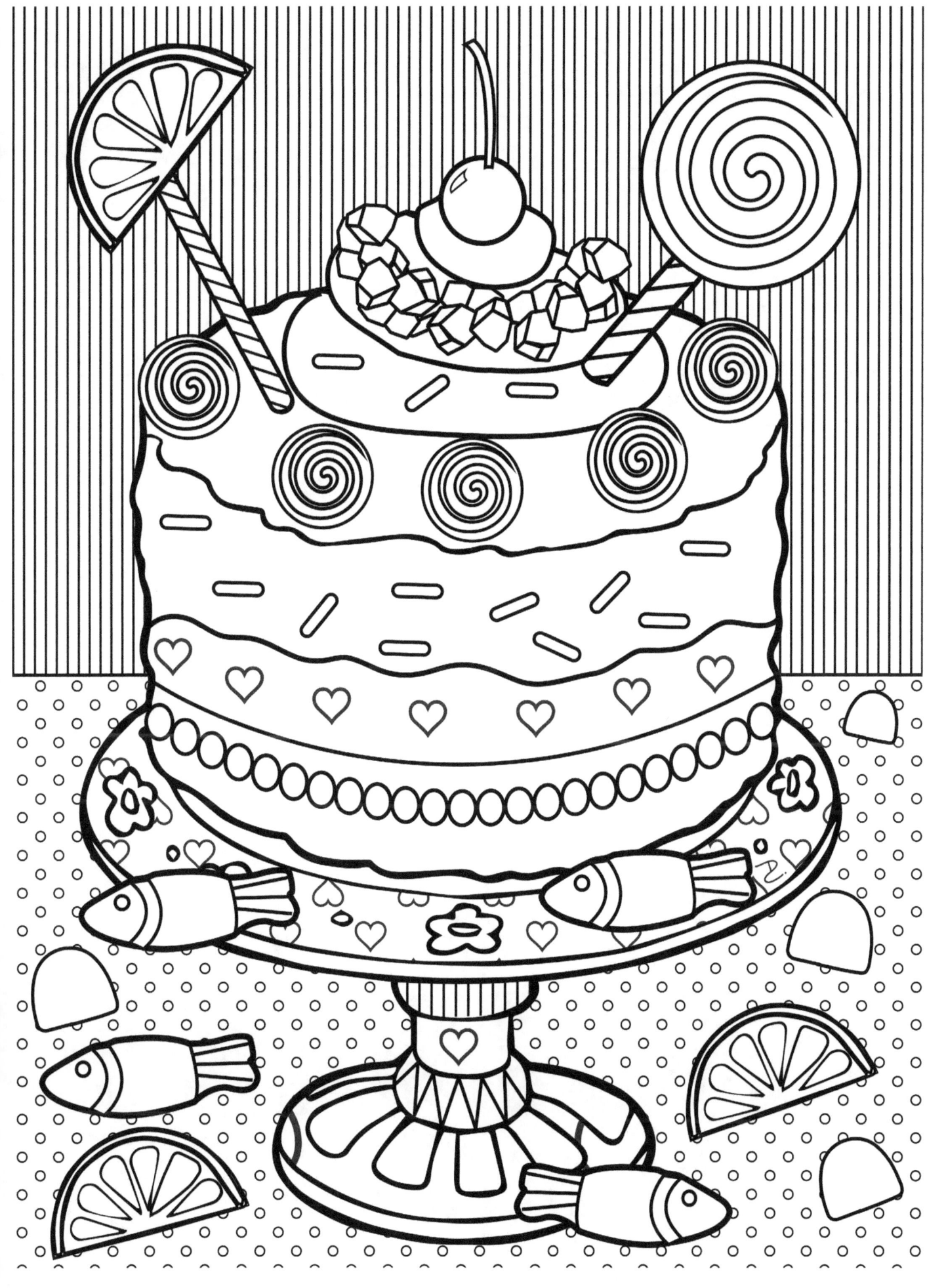

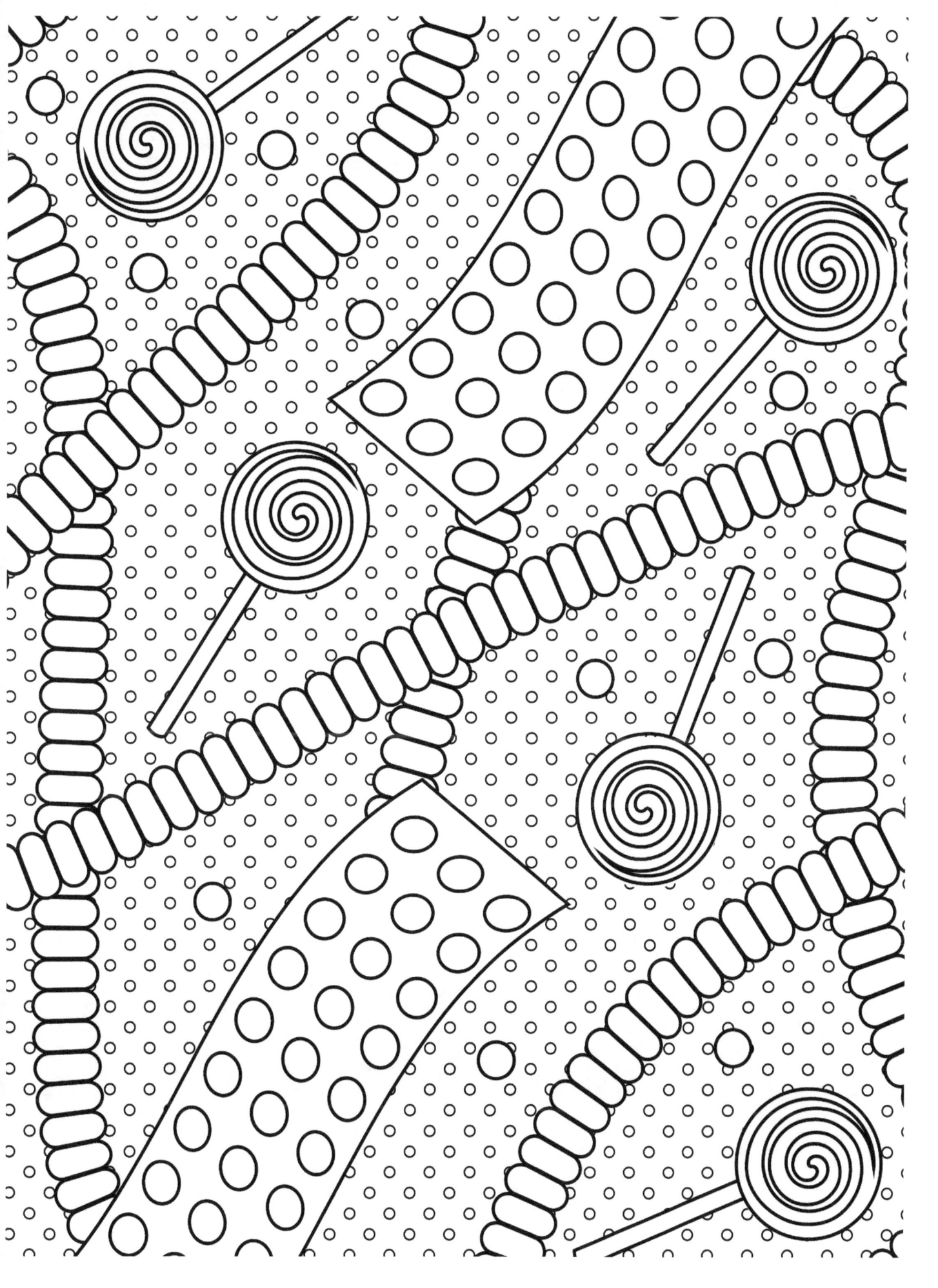

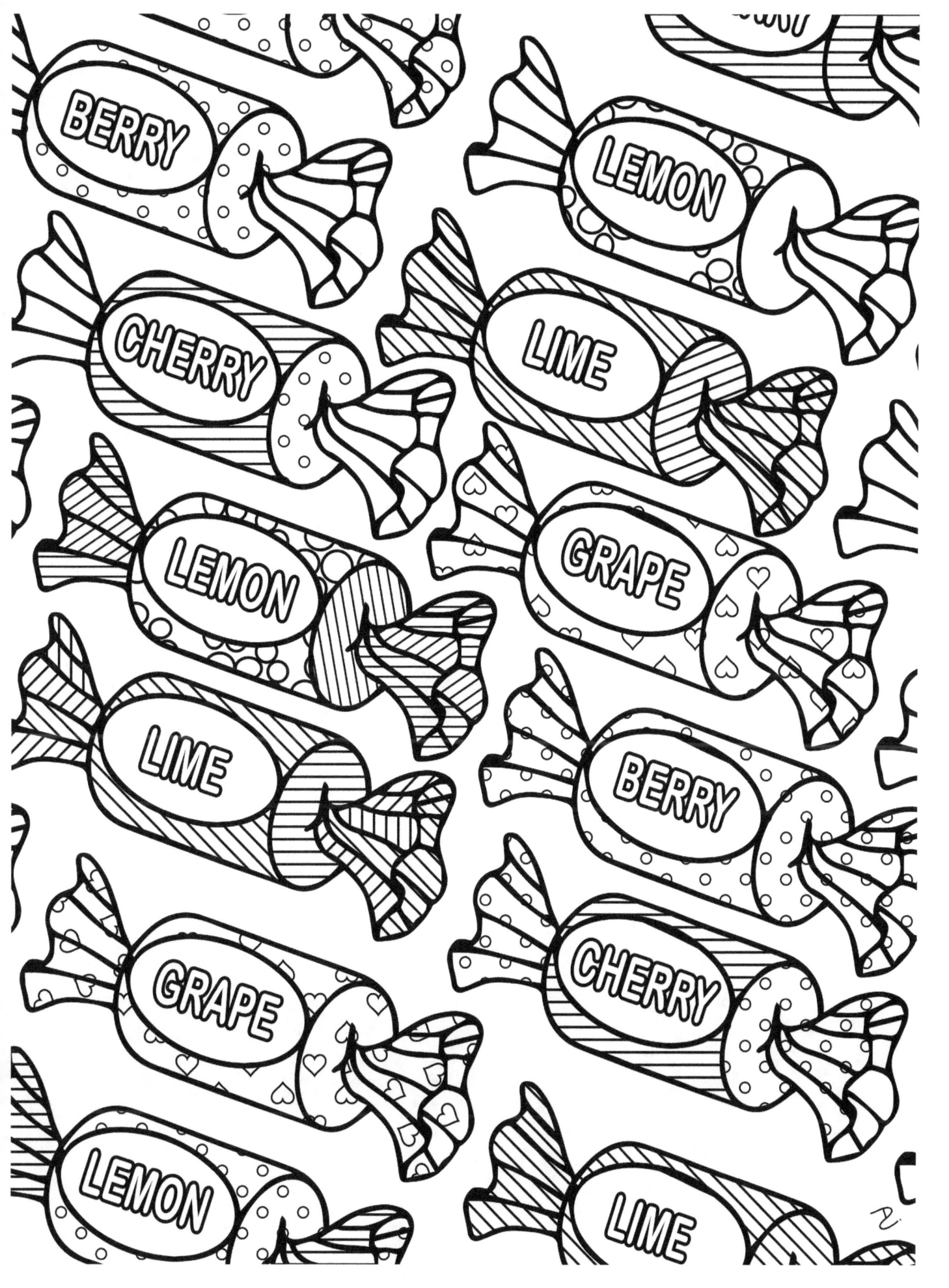

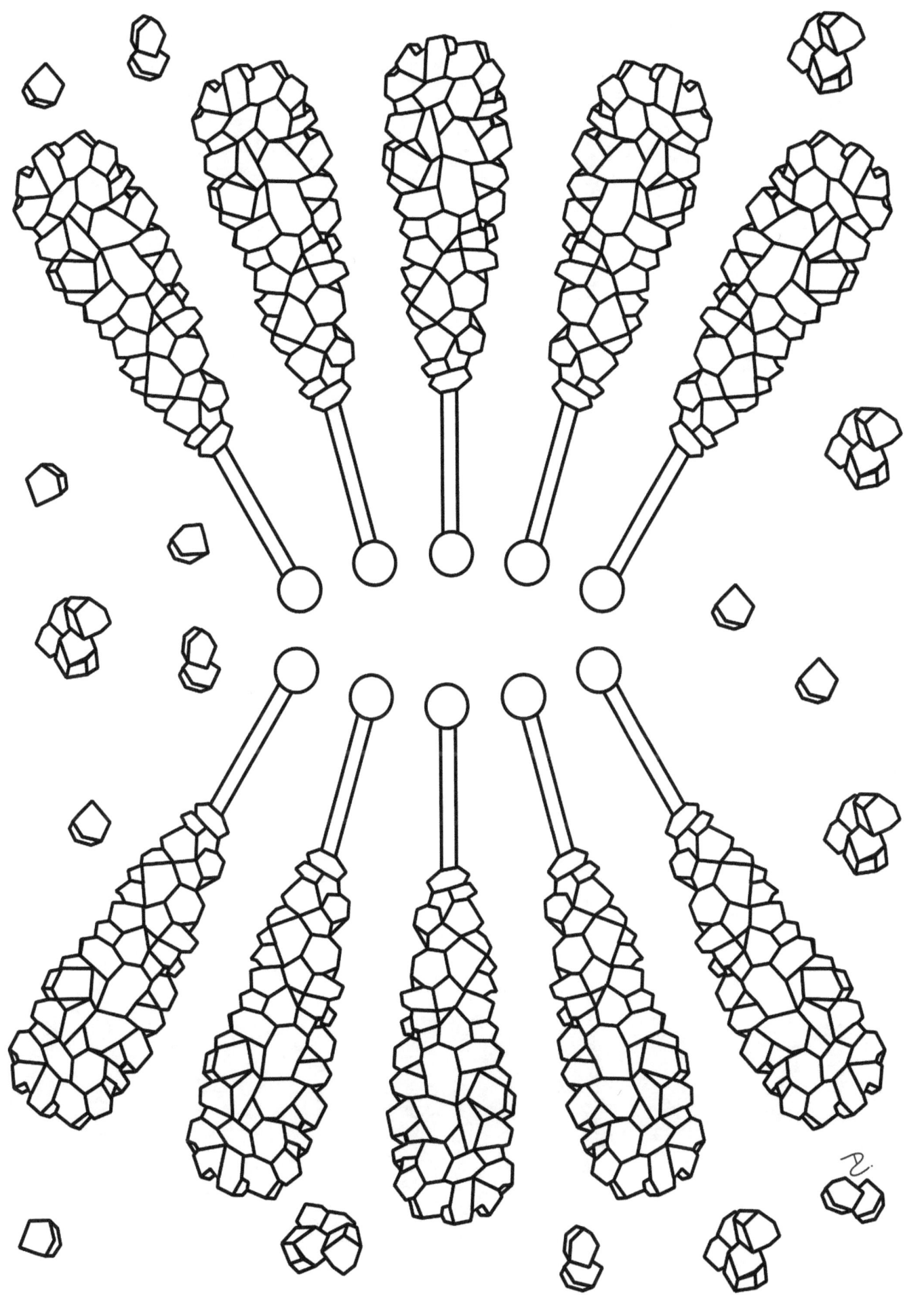

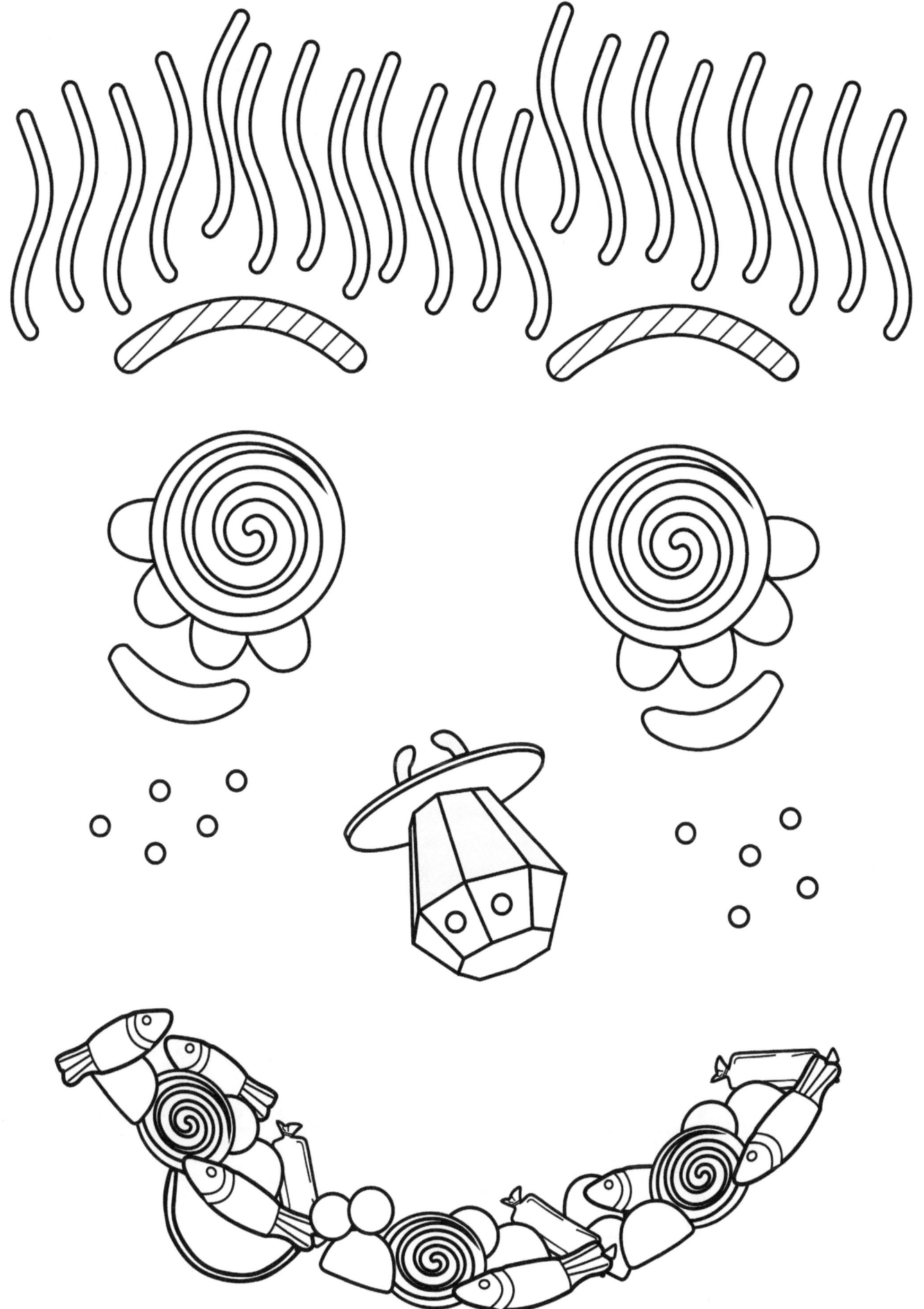

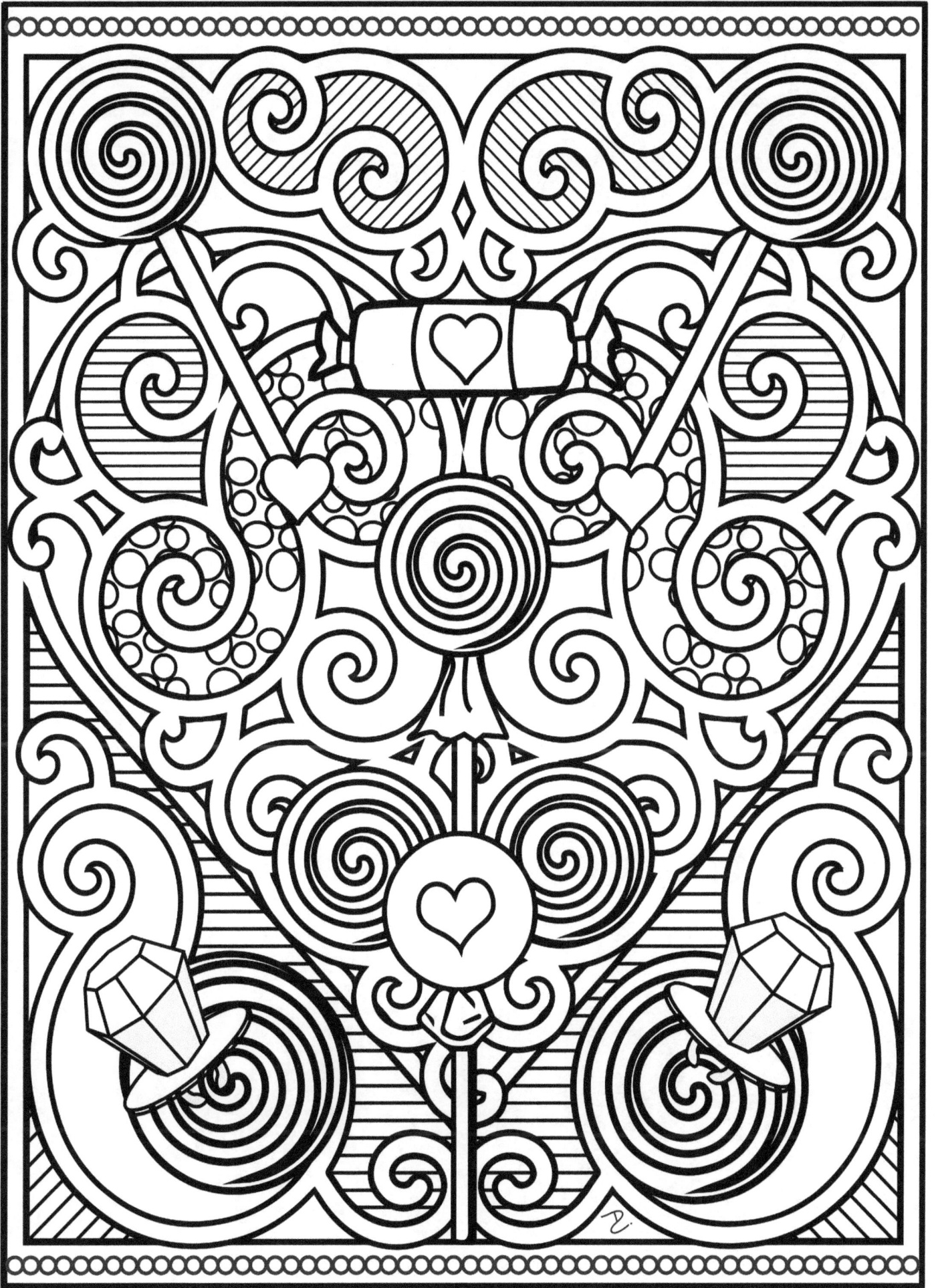

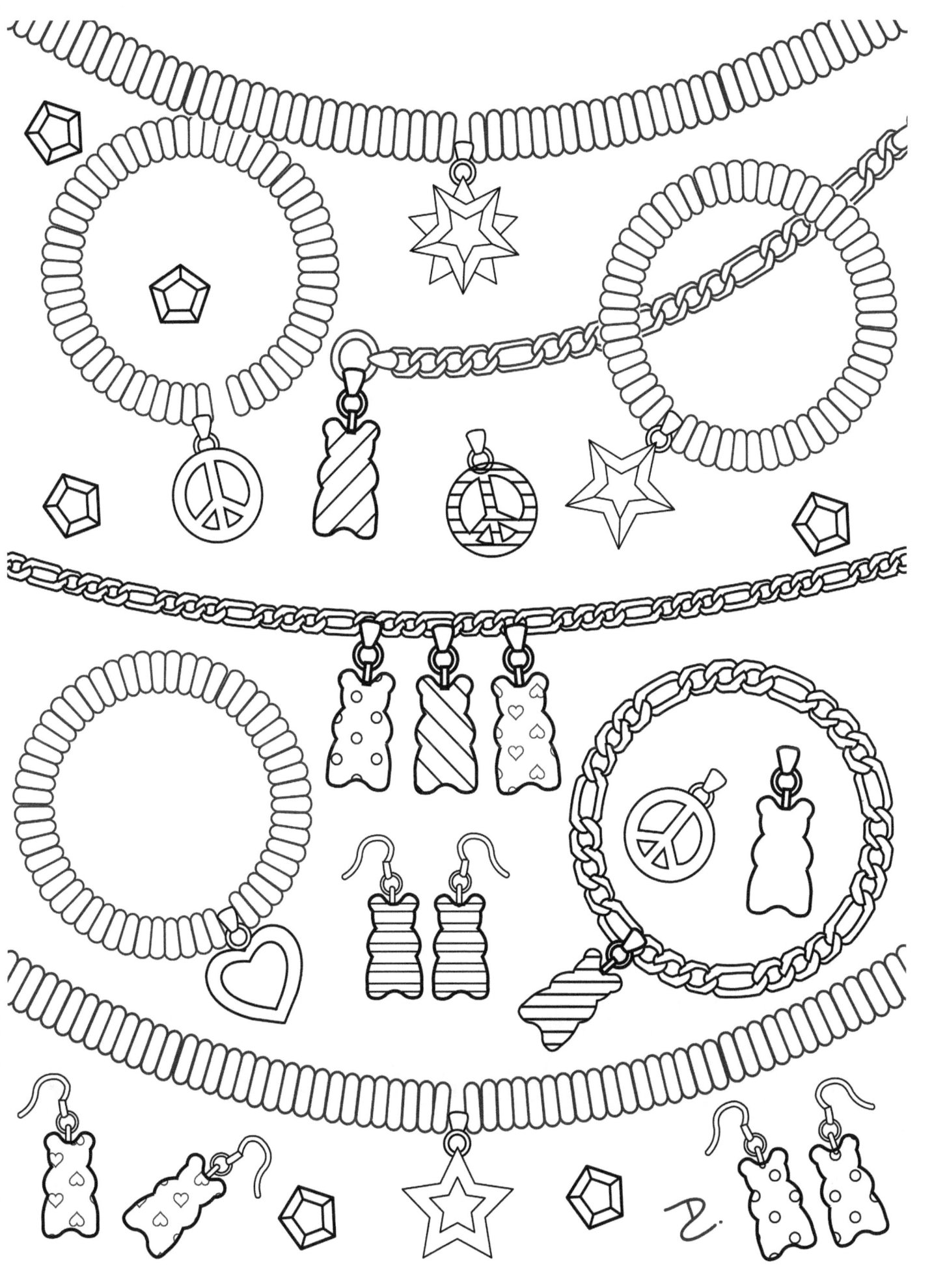

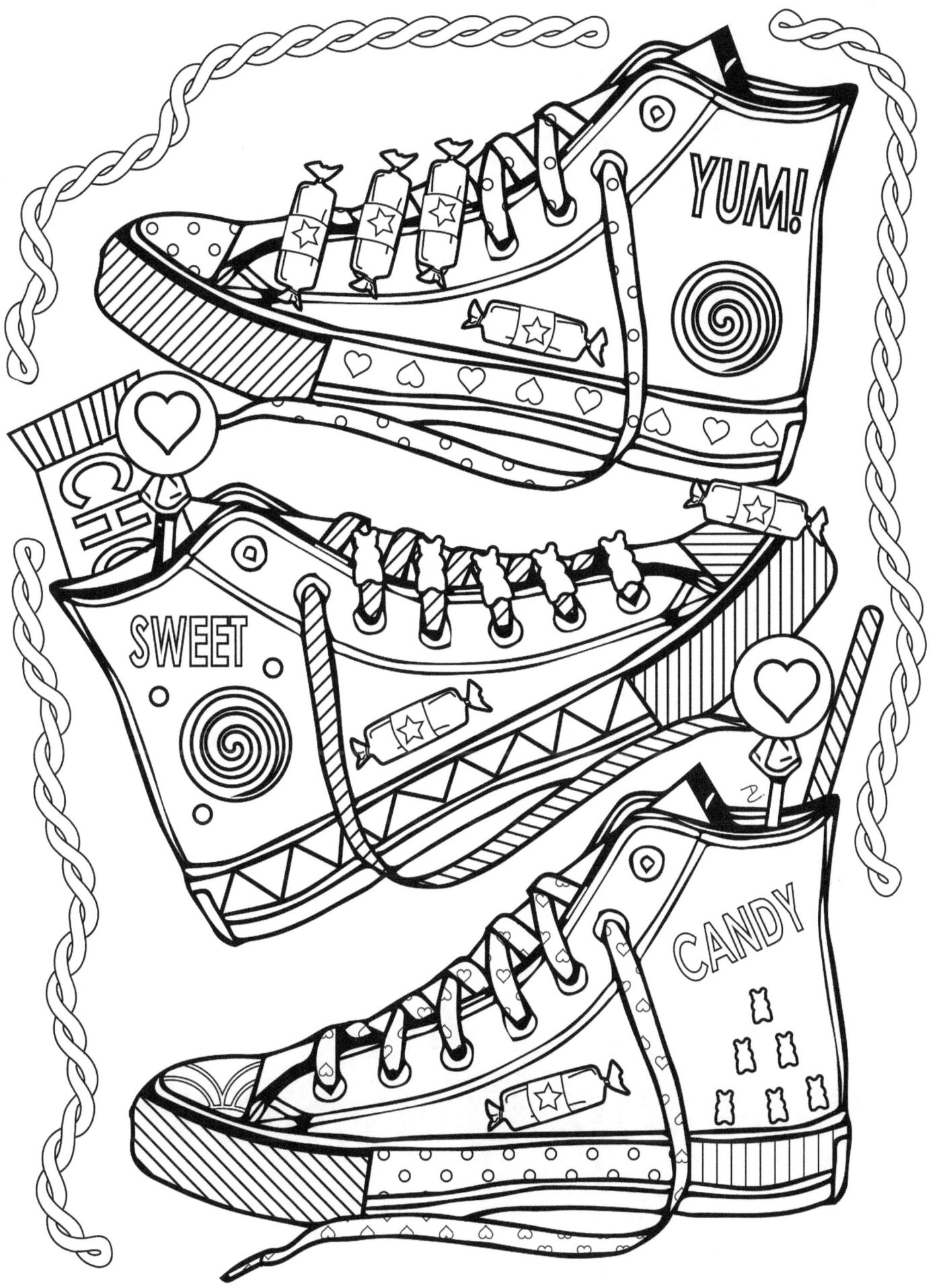

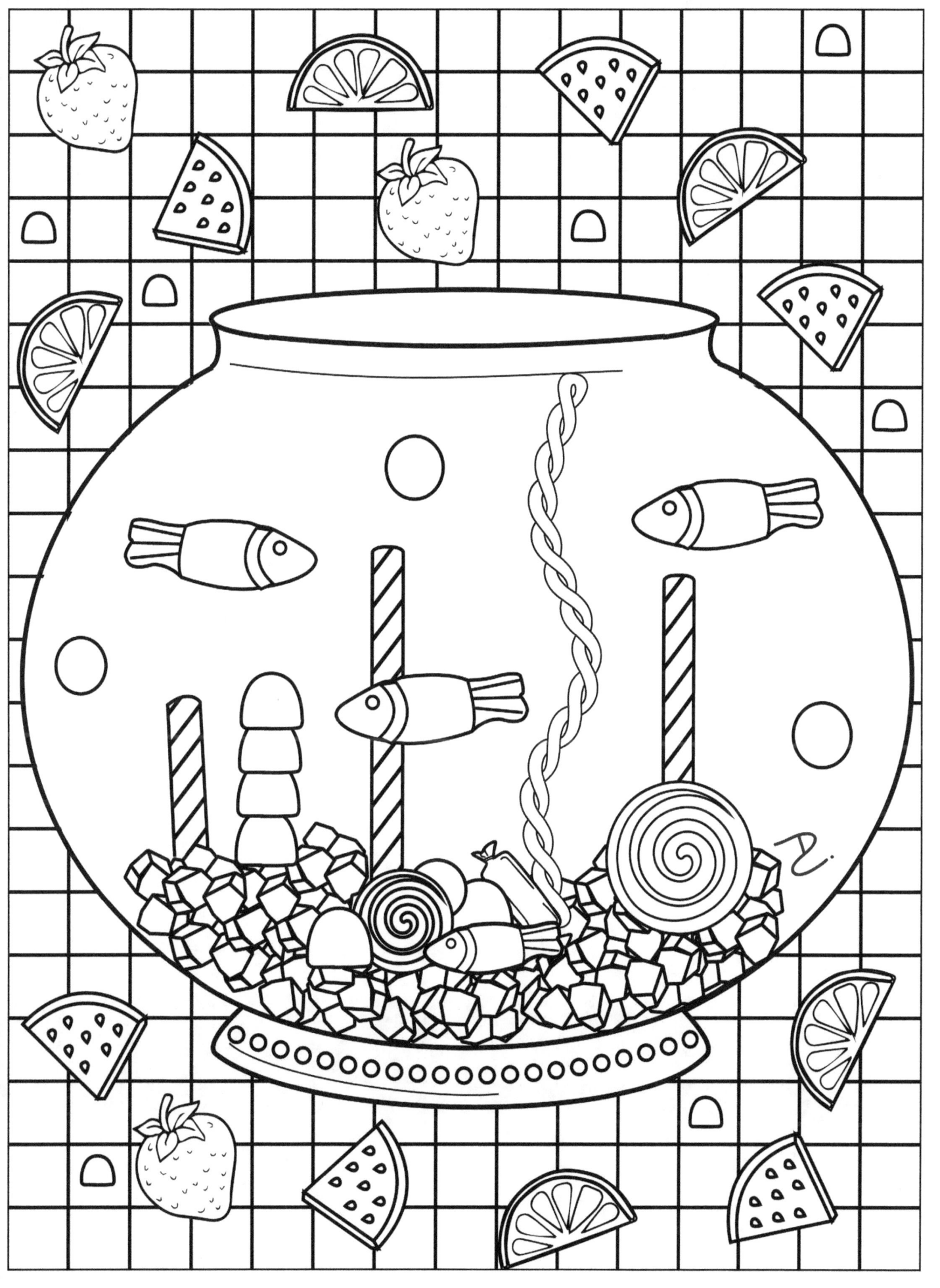

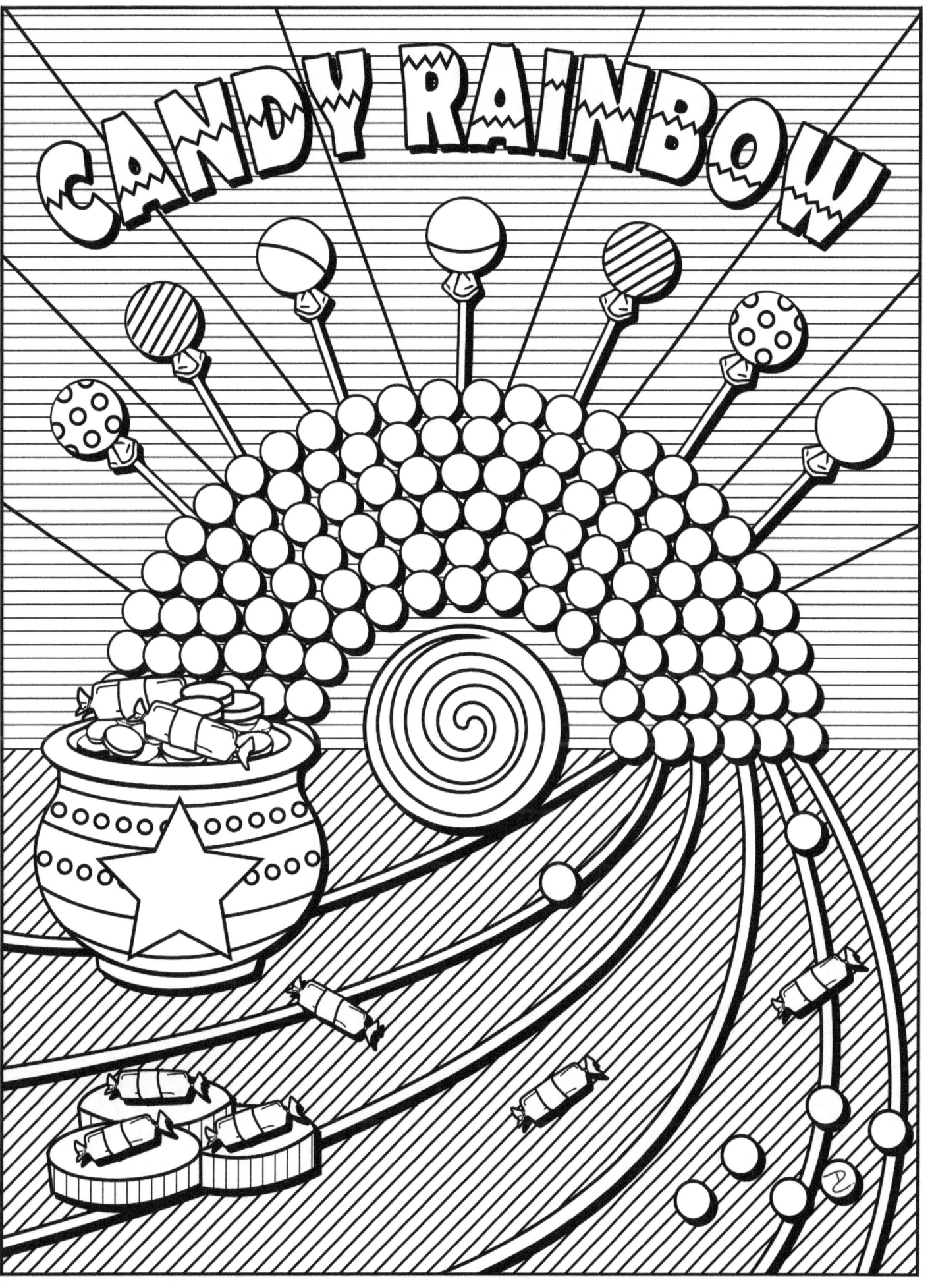

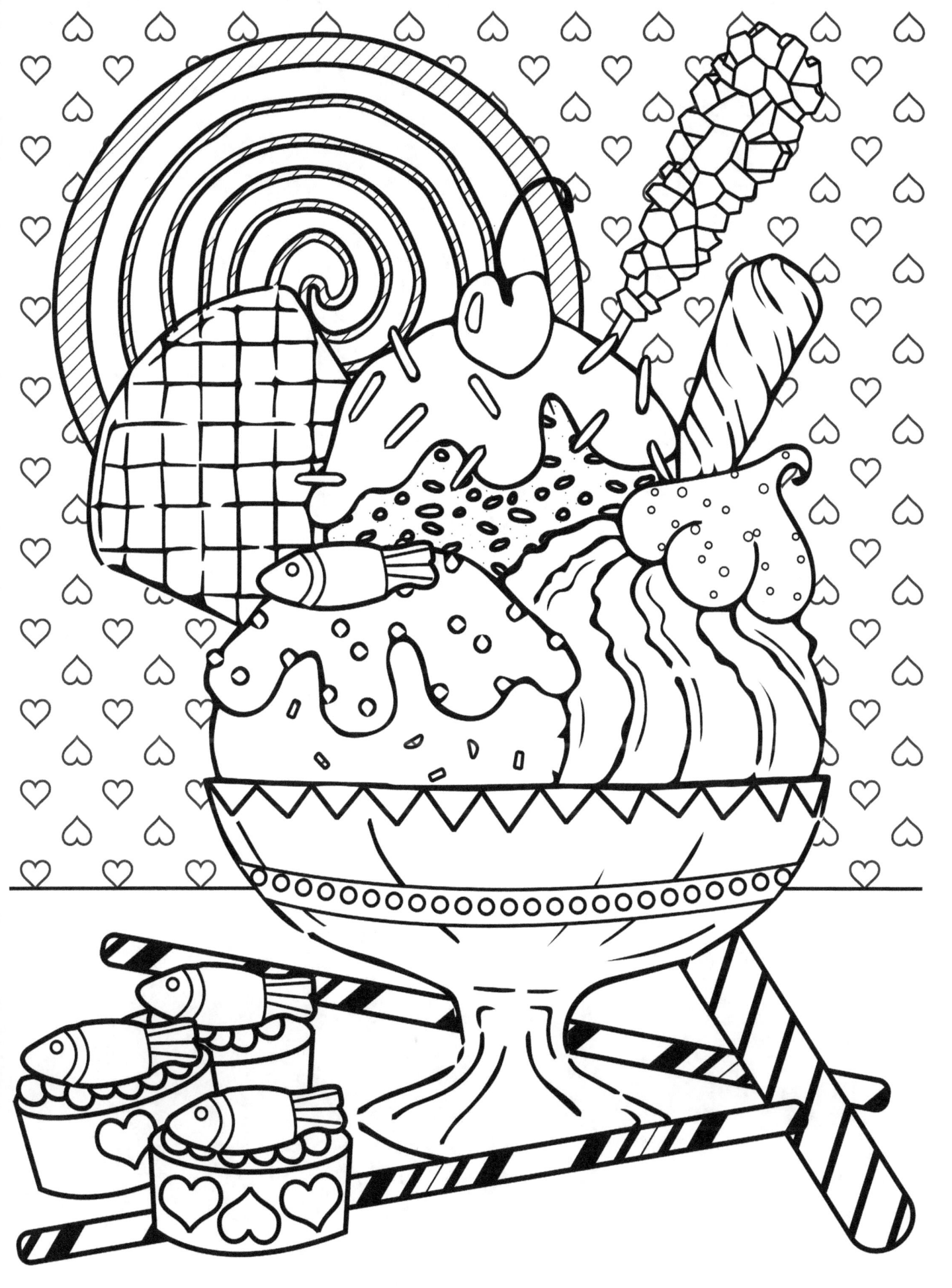

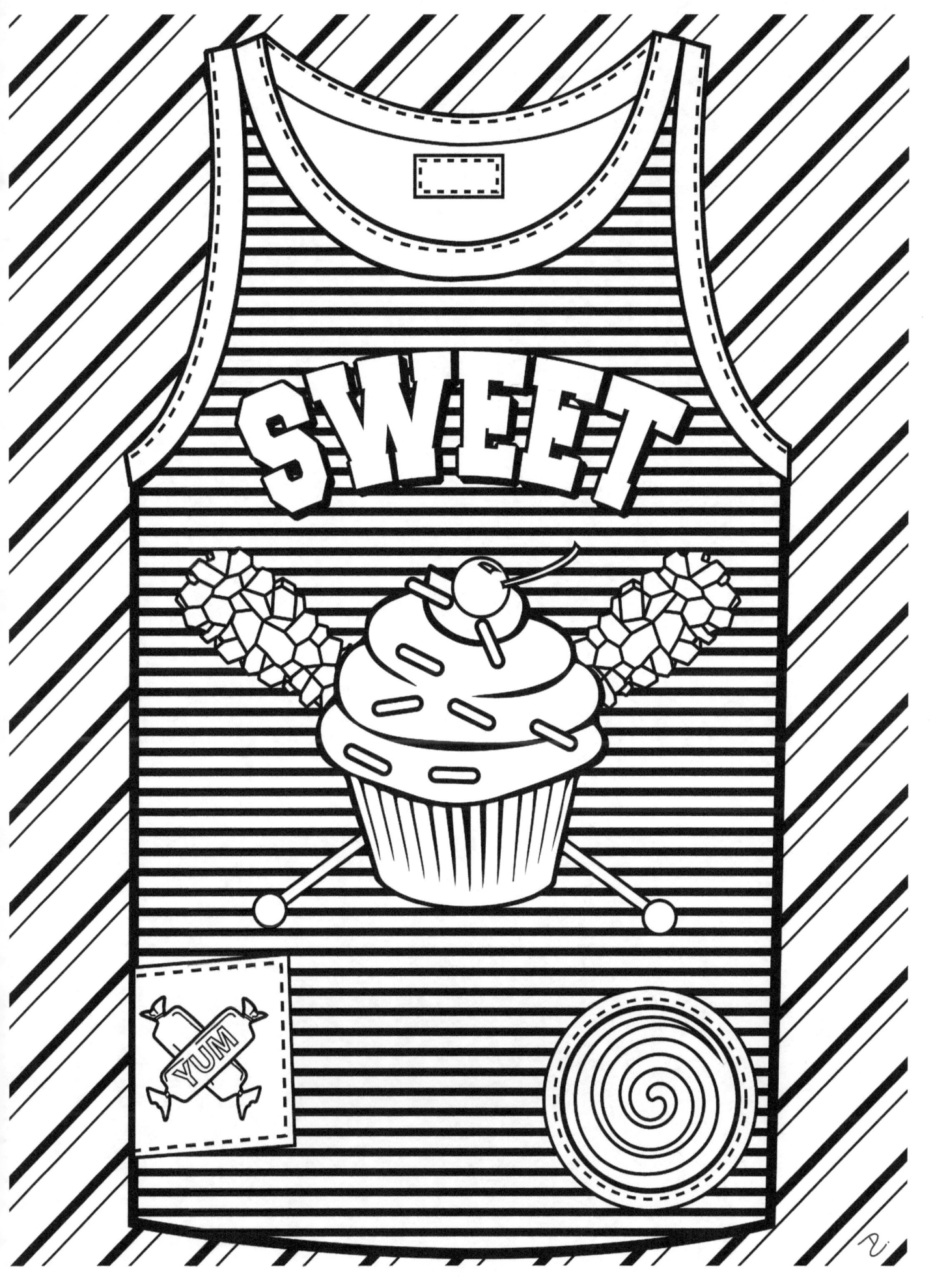

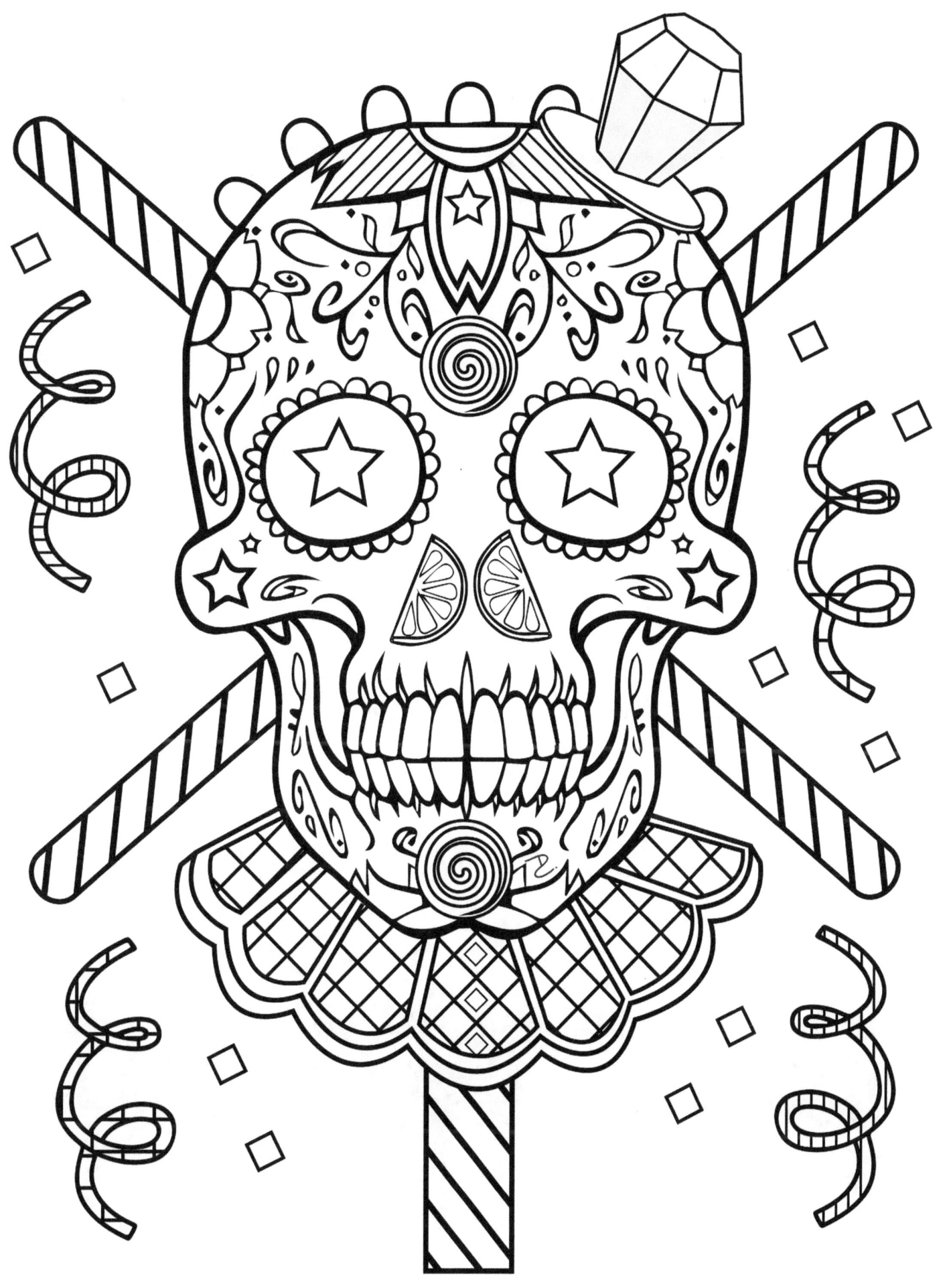

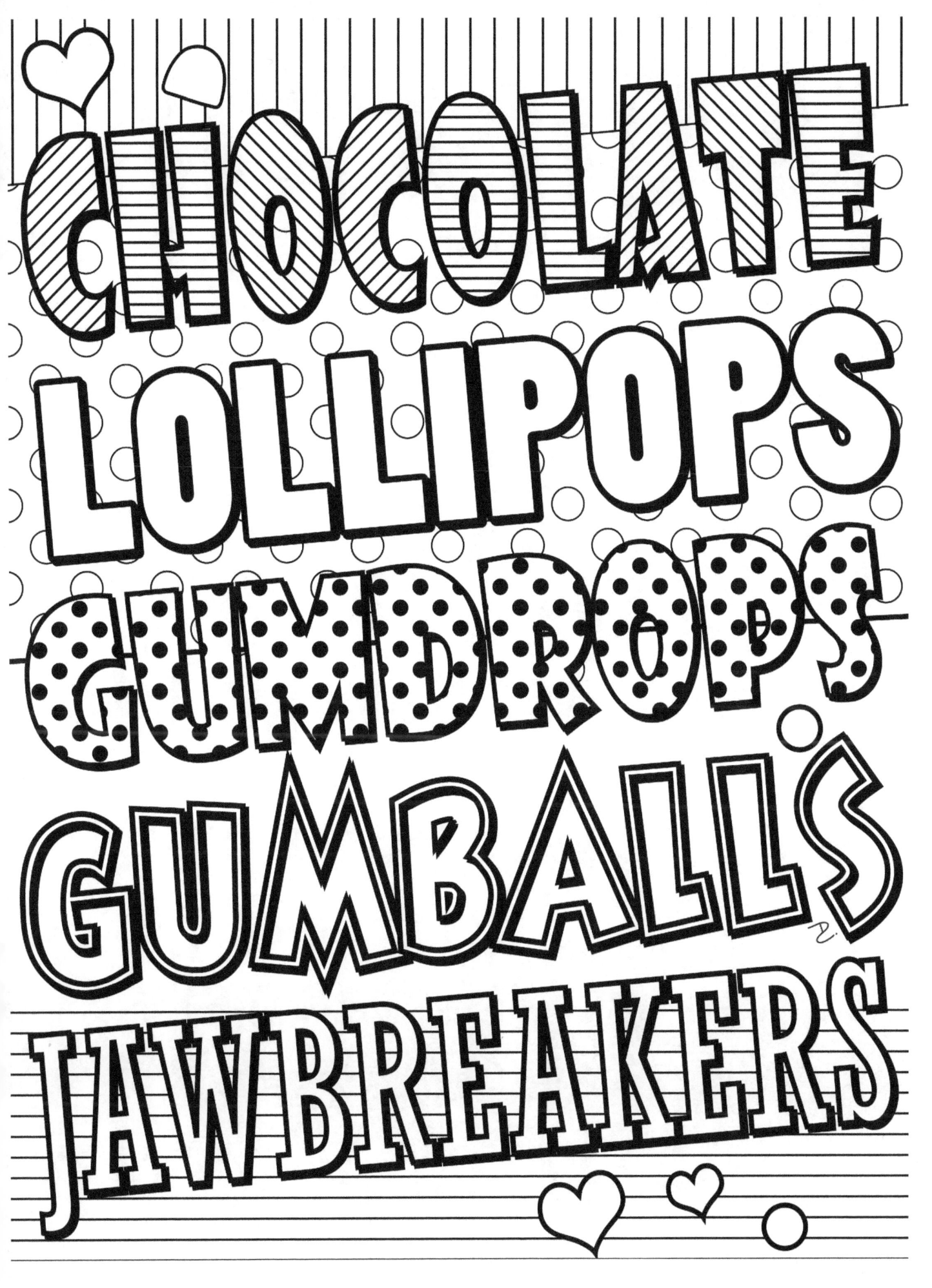

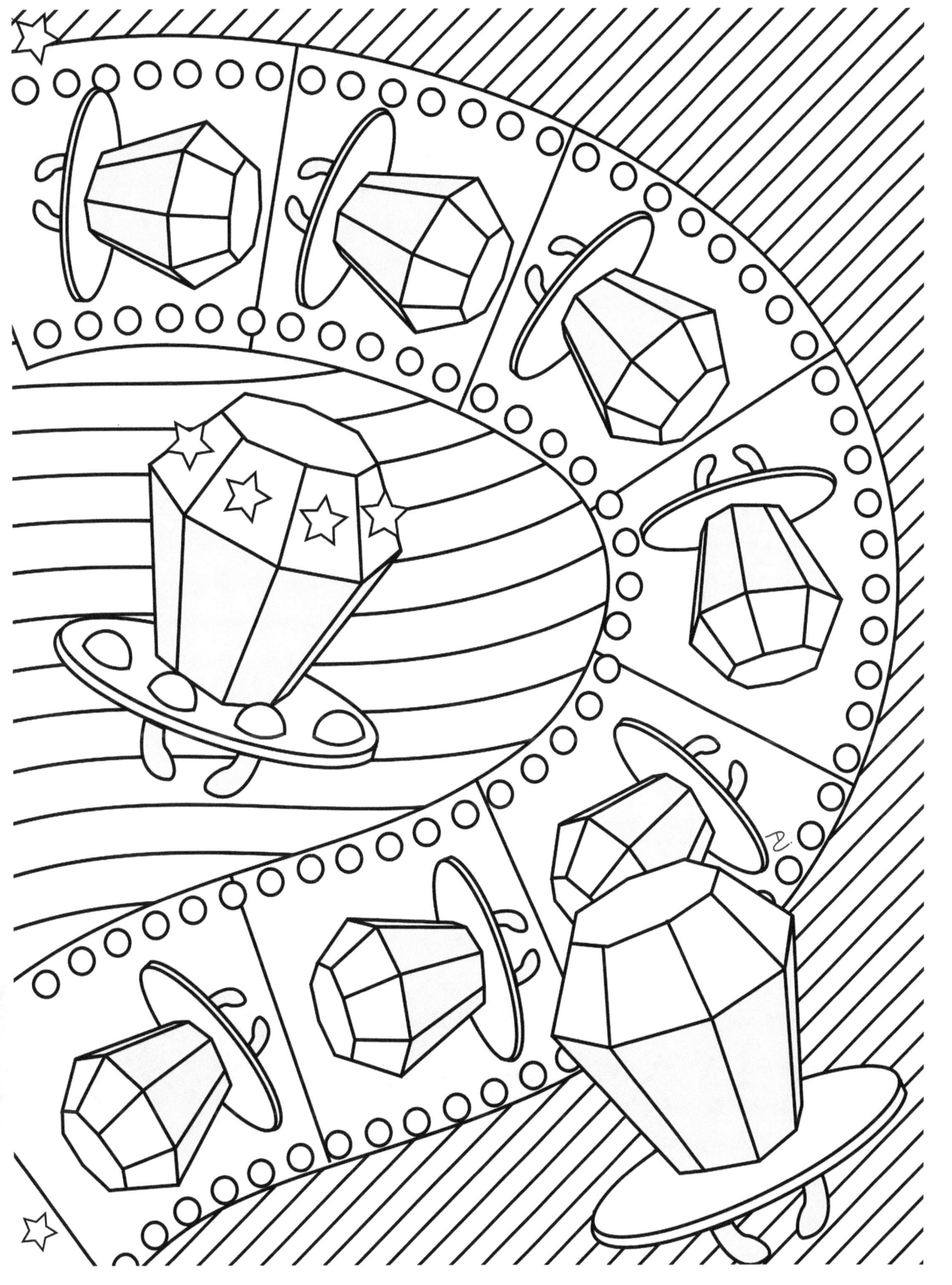

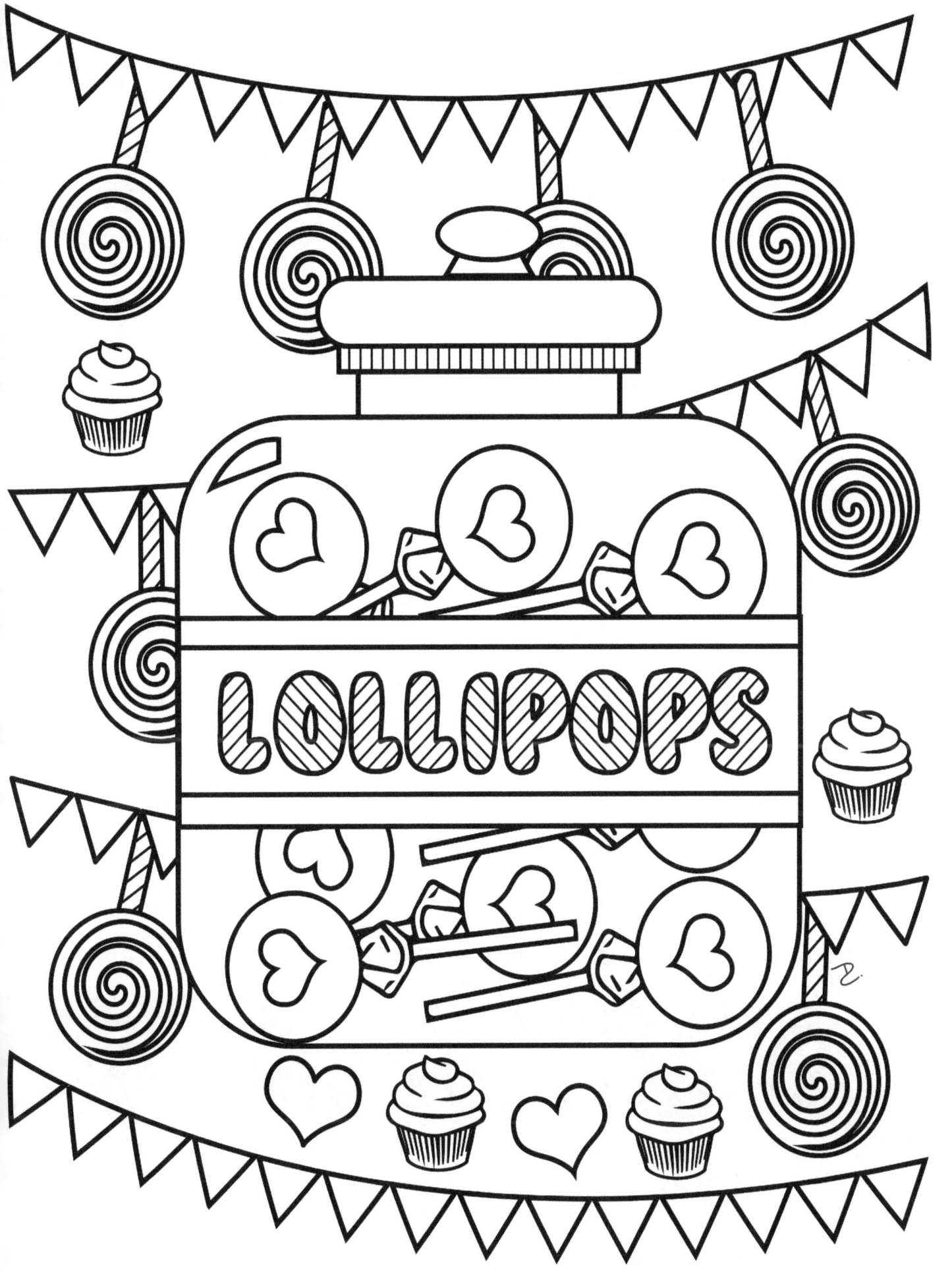

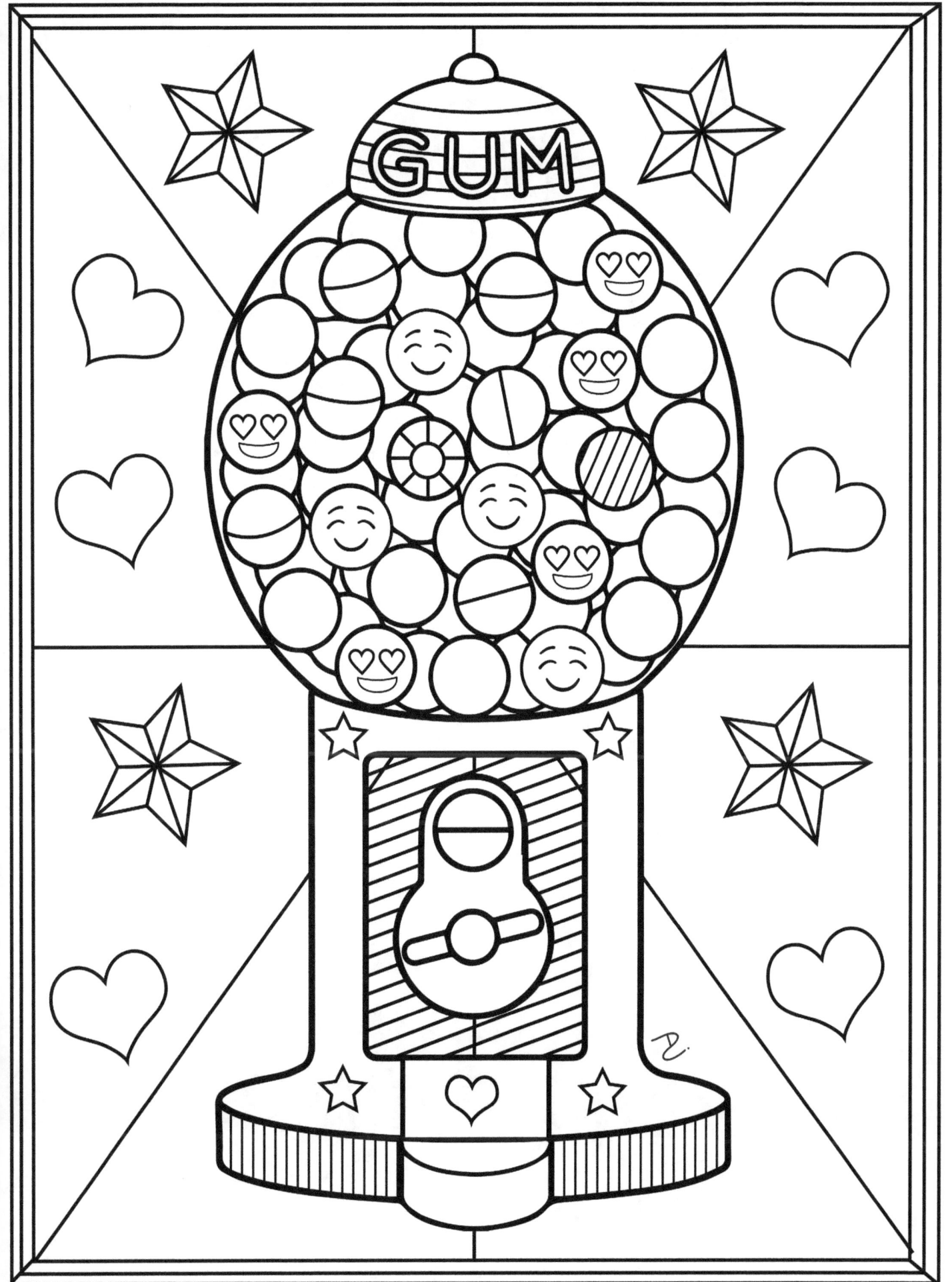

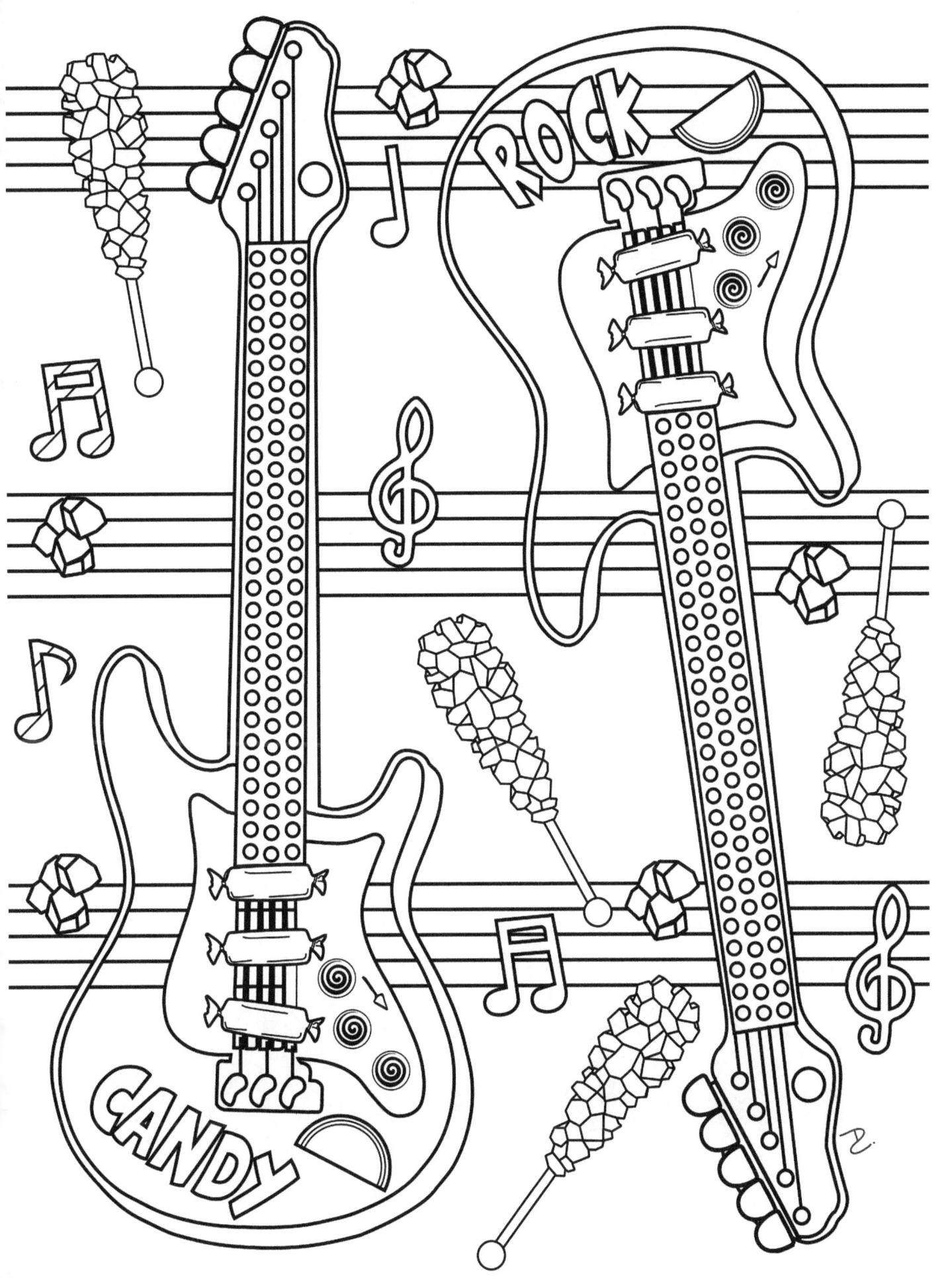

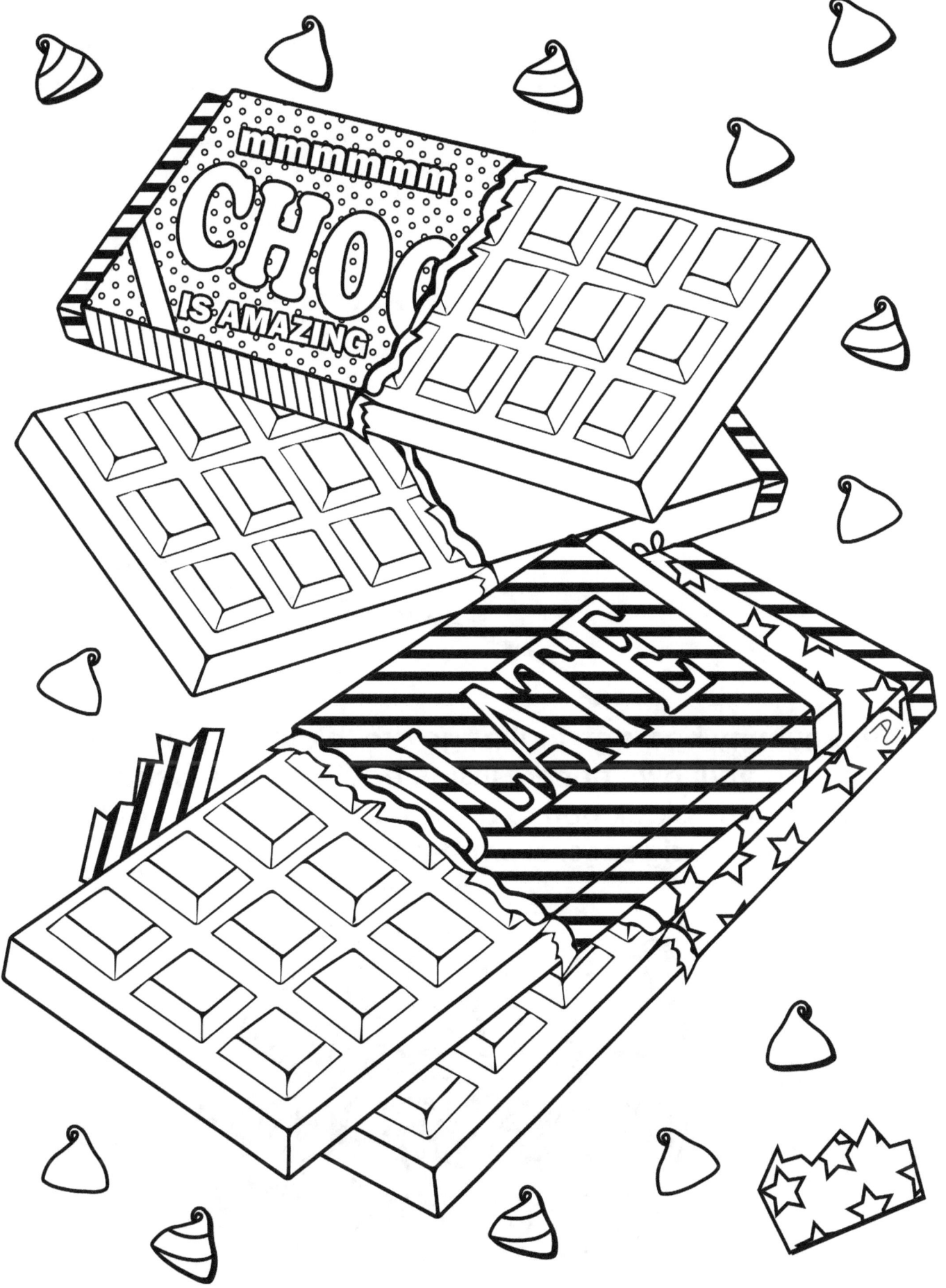

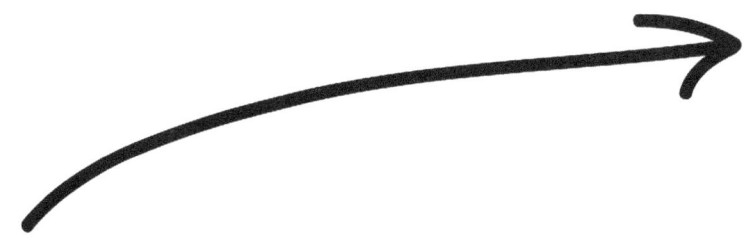

The gummy bears on that page are blank so you can try drawing your own pattern inside each gummy bear! Use a skinny black pen to draw some lines, polka dots, hearts, swirls, zig zags, or whatever else you want!!

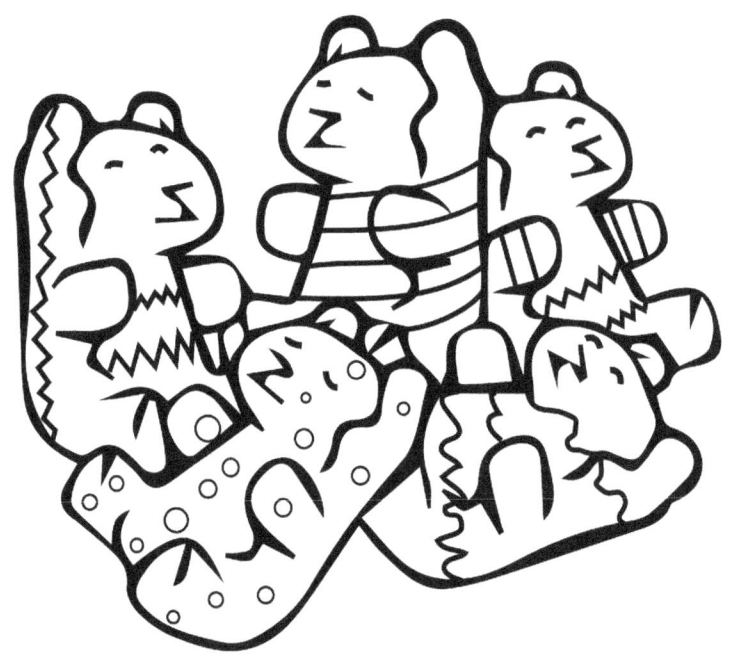

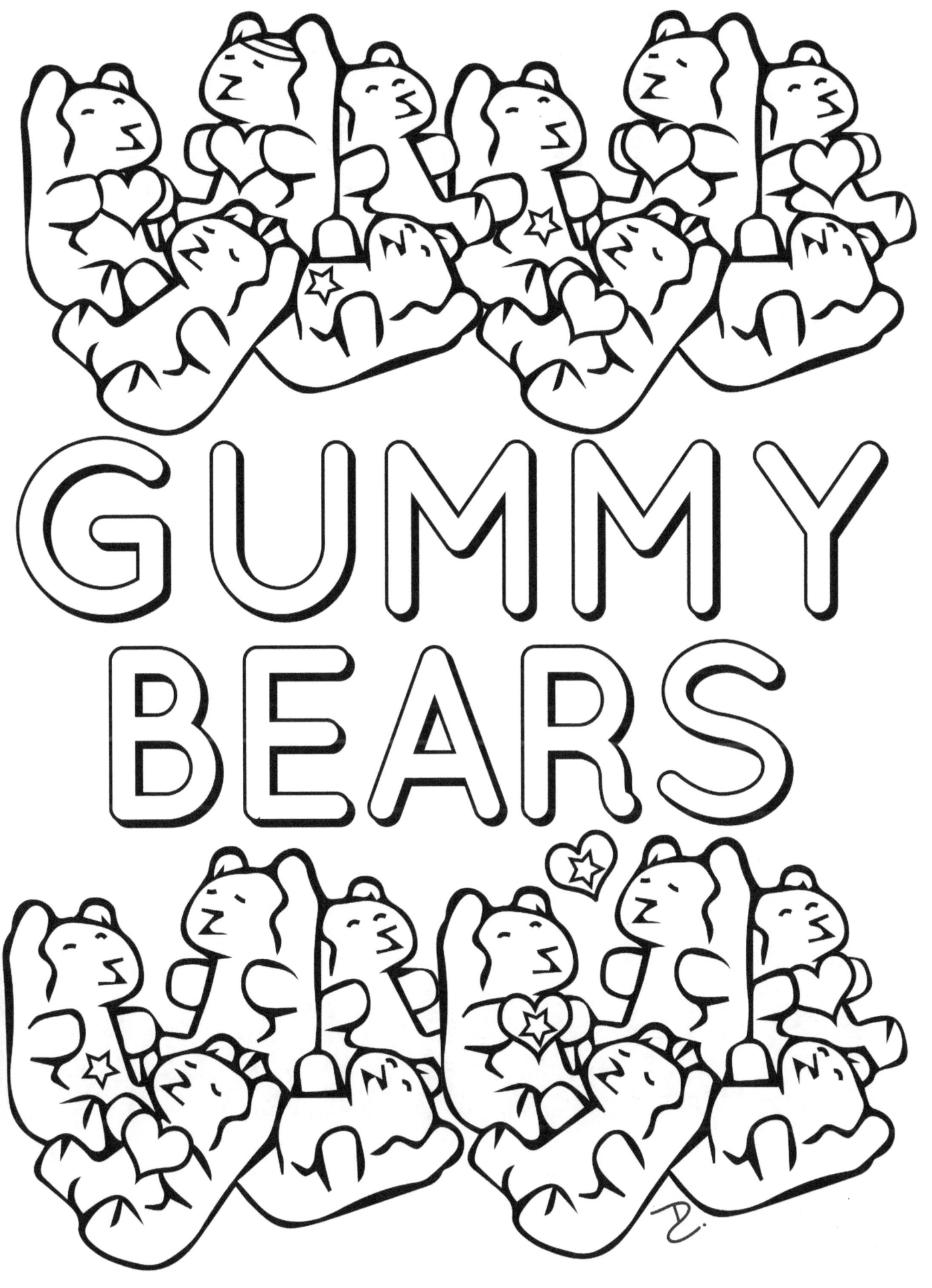